THE INWARD JOURNEY OF
ISAAC PENINGTON

AN ABBREVIATION OF PENINGTON'S WORKS

BY
ROBERT J. LEACH

PENDLE HILL PAMPHLET 29

He that readeth these things, let him not strive to comprehend them; but be content with what he feeleth thereof suitable to his own present estate, and as the life grows in him, and he in the life . . . the words . . . will of themselves open to him.

ISAAC PENINGTON

PENDLE HILL PAMPHLET 29

ISBN-87574-029-4
Library of Congress catalog card number 44-280

Printed in the United States of America by
Sowers Printing Company, Lebanon, Pa.

First printing 1944
Third printing July 1975: 1,500

INTRODUCTION

THE spiritual writings of Isaac Penington (1617-1679) evoke a real response in our present war-torn world. Their advice concerning the slow growth of inward comprehension speaks to our condition. Penington's many short pamphlets upon religious subjects were collected and published after the death of their author, in a folio volume entitled:

> The Works of the Long-Mournful and Sorely-Distressed Isaac Penington, whom the Lord in his Tender Mercy, at length Visited and Relieved by the Ministry of that Despised People, called Quakers; and in the Springings of that Light, Life and Holy Power in him, which they had Truly and Faithfully Testified of, and Directed his mind to, were these things Written, and are now Published as a thankful Testimony of the goodness of the Lord unto him, and for the Benefit of others.

This first edition, of 1681, has been several times republished and a number of books of selections have been edited. These are now out of print. For this reason the crystal-clear purity of Isaac Penington's heavenly cadences is scarcely available to any but scholars.

The *Inward Journey of Isaac Penington* is an abbreviation of the 1,400 pages of the second London edition of 1761. The extracted portions have been joined to form a sequence. The deepest questions are asked and answered: What of thee? Art thou in thine own soul's true rest? What is the seed, or portion of God in every heart? What of free will, justification, perfection, and more especially, love, joy, and peace? The lyric beauty of Penington's free verse carries the reader along to the subject of public worship, in which Christ himself speaks.

Half of Isaac Penington's twenty-two Quaker years were spent in prison—"in outward bonds for Christ's sake." At first hand he knew of the blessed community, of the persecuting spirit, and of men's dependence upon war and violence. After dealing with Quaker testimonies, the *Inward Journey* recapitulates the steps by which all may find the living virtue which Isaac Penington had himself discovered and which brought him the sense of salvation.

A few additional facts concerning Penington's life should be noted. Born in 1617, son of Alderman Isaac Penington, a distinguished Puritan who was at one time Lord Mayor of London, he received an excellent education which was reflected in his able use of the English tongue. A fashionable fling in London society eventuated in his marriage to Lady Mary Springett whose daughter by a prior marriage was later to become the wife of William Penn. In 1658 the Peningtons, who had long been religious seekers, fully associated themselves with the then new Society of Friends. Rejecting their worldly advantages, they became consistent and fervent members of the new spiritual movement. As public Friends and ministers of God's holy word, Isaac Penington and his wife travelled in the company of James Naylor, George Keith, William Penn, George Fox, and Robert Barclay. In the *Inward Journey* we participate in this flood-tide of Christian experience. We become "tinctured" by the authenticity of the witness that is here recorded. We should be, in a measure, revitalized by means of Isaac Penington's heavenly words.

ROBERT J. LEACH

Camp Pocomoke,
Civilian Public Service.

1

THE SPRING OF LIFE

I WAS acquainted with a spring of life from my child-hood, which enlightened me in my tender years and pointed my heart towards the Lord, begetting true sense in me, and faith, and hope, and love, and humility, and meekness, . . . so that indeed I was a wonder to some that knew me, because of the savor and life of religion which dwelt in my heart and appeared in my conversation.

But I never durst trust the spring of my life, . . . but, in reading the Scriptures, gathered what knowledge I could therefrom, and set this over the spring and springings of life in me, and indeed judged that I ought so to do.

Indeed, I did not look to have been so broken, shattered, and distressed as I afterwards was, and could by no means understand the meaning thereof, . . . not having the sense of any guilt upon me. Divers came to see me, some to enquire into, and consider of, my condition; others to bewail it and (if possible) administer some relief, help, and comfort to me; and divers were the judgments they had concerning me. Some would say it was deep melancholy; others would narrowly search and enquire how, and in what manner, . . . I had walked; and were jealous that I had sinned against the Lord and provoked him some way or other, and that some iniquity lay as a load upon me; but, after thorough converse with me, they would still express that they were of another mind and that the hand of the Lord was in it, . . . and it would end in good to my soul.

When I was broken and dashed to pieces in my religion, I was in a congregational way; but soon after parted with them, yet in great love, relating to them how the hand of the Lord was upon me, and how I was smitten in the inward part of my religion, and could not now hold up an outward form of that which I inwardly wanted, having lost my God, my Christ, my faith, my knowledge, my life, my all. And so we parted very lovingly, I wishing them well, even the presence of that God whom I wanted; promising to return to them again, if ever I met with that which my soul wanted, and had clearness in the Lord so to do.

In this great trouble and grief, . . . and in mourning over and grappling with secret corruptions and temptations, I spent many years. and fell into great weakness of body; and often casting myself upon my bed, did wring my hands and weep bitterly, begging earnestly of the Lord, daily, that I might be pitied by him, and helped against my enemies, and be made conformable to the image of his Son, by his own renewing power. And indeed at last (when my nature was almost spent, and the pit of despair was even closing its mouth upon me) mercy sprang, and deliverance came, and the Lord my God owned me, and sealed his love unto me, and light sprang within me, which made not only the Scriptures. but the very outward creatures glorious in my eye, so that everything was sweet and pleasant and lightsome round about me. But I soon felt that this estate was too high and glorious for me, and I was not able to abide in it, it so overcame my natural spirits; wherefore, blessing the name of the Lord for his great goodness to me, I prayed unto him to take that from me which I was not able to bear, and to give me such a proportion of his light and presence as was suitable to my present state, and might fit me for his service. Whereupon this was presently removed from me, yet a savor remained with me, wherein I had sweetness, and comfort, and refreshment for a long season.

"Well then, how came this about?" will some say.

Why thus. The Lord opened my spirit, the Lord gave me the certain and sensible feeling of the pure seed, which had been with me from the beginning; the Lord caused his holy power to fall upon me, and gave me such an inward demonstration and feeling of the seed of life, that I cried out in my spirit, *This is he, this is he; there is not another, there never was another. He was always near me, though I knew him not. . . . Oh! that I might now be joined to him, and he alone might live in me.* And so in the willingness which God had wrought in me. . . I gave up to be instructed, exercised, and led by him, in the waiting for and feeling of his holy seed, that all might be wrought out of me which could not live with the seed . . . . And so I have gone through a sore travail and fight of afflictions and temptations of many kinds, wherein the Lord hath been merciful to me in helping me and preserving the spark of life in me, in the midst of many things which had befallen me, whose nature tended to quench and extinguish it.

Now thus having met with the true way . . . I cannot be silent (true love and pure life stirring in me and moving me), but am necessitated to testify of it to others;

and this is it: to retire inwardly, and wait to feel somewhat of the Lord, somewhat of his holy spirit and power, discovering and drawing from that which is contrary to him, and into his holy nature and heavenly image.

The main thing in religion is to receive a principle of life from God, whereby the mind may be changed, and the heart made able to understand the mysteries of his kingdom, and to see and walk in the way of life; and this is the travail of the souls of the righteous, that they may abide, grow up, and walk with the Lord in this principle; and that others also, who breathe after him, may be gathered into, and feel the virtue of, the same principle.

But there is one that stands in the way to hinder this work of the Lord, who with great subtility strives to keep souls in captivity, and to prejudice them against the precious living appearances of the redeeming power of the Lord.

One great way whereby he doth this is, by raising up in them a fear lest they should be deceived and betrayed, and instead of obtaining more, lose that little of God which they have. With this was I exercised long; and still, when life stirred in my heart, then this fear was raised in me; so that I durst not in judgment close with what secretly in spirit I felt to be of God, it having a true touch of his quickening, warming, convincing, enlivening virtue in it.

Now, he that would meet with the true religion, the religion of the gospel, must meet with the power, receive the power, believe, dwell, and act in the power. For Christ was made a king, a priest, and prophet, not after the law of a carnal commandment, but after the power of an endless life: and his covenant is not like the old, in word or letter; but in the same power and life wherein the priests were made ministers.

So the knowledge here, the faith here, the hope here . . . are not literal, but living. He that receiveth this knowledge, receiveth living knowledge. This faith gives victory over unbelief, and over that spirit whose strength lies in unbelief. This hope purifies the heart even as he is pure. And he that receiveth the righteousness of this covenant, receiveth a living garment, which hath power in it over death and unrighteousness. The beginning of this religion, of this power and holy inward covenant, is sweet; but the pure progress and going on of it much more pleasant, as the Lord gives to feel the growth and sweet living freshness of it; notwithstanding the temptations, fears, troubles, trials, oppositions, and great dangers, both within and without, . . . all its ways are pleasantness, and its paths peace; yea, the very yoke is easy and the burden light, when the mind and will is changed by the power, and helped and assisted by the Lord in its subjection to the power.

The Lord is now gentle and tender, pursuing thee with his love, and following thee up and down with his light. And though thou run from him into sin and transgression, and hearken to the wisdom of the flesh, yet his voice comes after thee to reclaim thee; and if thou wilt hear, and but yield thyself to him, he will not put thee to do any thing, but subdue all thy enemies for thee; yea, he will slay the serpentine wisdom in thee, with all its inventions, and dash all the children of Babylon against the stones, without pity to them, though with great pity to thee.

[5]

Therefore take heed of the fleshly wisdom; take heed of thine own understanding; take heed of thy reasoning or disputing; for these are the weapons wherewith the witness is slain. That wisdom must be destroyed, and that understanding brought to naught, and thou become a child, and learn as a child if ever thou know the things of God.

Yea, theie are some who are grievously sick in soul, and deeply wounded in spirit, the sadness and misery of whose condition cries aloud for the help of the physician. Now the eye and heart of the Lord is more especially towards these; and so he bids his prophets be instructing and comforting these, concerning the salvation, the healing, the oil of gladness, the Messiah to come; and when he comes, he sends him up and down to seek out these, to keep company with these, to help and relieve these; having given him the tongue of the learned, to speak a word in season to these weary distressed ones. These are not like the common, rough, unhewn, knotty, rugged earth; but like earth prepared for the seed, and so easily and naturally receive it. The gospel is preached to others at a distance; which, it is true, they may have, if they will hearken to it, and wait for it, and part with what must first be parted with; but they have a great way to travel thither. But these are near the kingdom; these are near that which opens, and lets in life; these are quickly reached to, melted, and brought into the sense in which with joy they receive the faith, and with the faith the power which brings righteousness and salvation to their souls.

2

FAITH

THERE is a faith which is of a man's self, and a faith which is the gift of God; or, a power of believing which is found in the nature of fallen man, and a power of believing which is given from above. As there are two births, the first and the second, so they have each their faith, . . . and seem to lay hold on the same thing for life; and the contention about the inheritance will not be ended, till God determine it.

Therefore observe and consider well, what this faith which is of a man's self can do; and how far it may go in the changing of man, and in producing a conformity of him to the letter of the Scriptures. And then consider where it is shut out, what it cannot do, what change it cannot make, and what it cannot conform to, that so the true distinction may be let into the mind, and not a foundation laid of so great a mistake in a matter of so great concernment.

A man may believe the history of the Scriptures, yea, and all the doctrines of them (so far as he can reach them with his understanding) with this faith which is of man . . . As by this faith a man can receive doctrines of instruction out of philosophers' books, so by the same faith he may receive doctrines of instructions out of the Scriptures. . . .

This being believed from the relation of the history

of these things, it naturally sets all the powers of man on work . . . towards the avoiding of misery and the attaining of happiness. . . . Must he pray? He will pray. Must he hear? He will hear. Must he read? He will read. Must he meditate? He will meditate. Must he deny himself and all his own righteousness and duties, and hope only for salvation in the merits of Christ? He will seem to do that too, and say, when he has done all he can, he is but an unprofitable servant. Does the Scripture say he can do nothing without the Spirit? He will acknowledge that too, and he hopes he has the Spirit. . . . Thus man by a natural faith grows up and spreads into a great tree, and is very confident and much pleased, not perceiving the defect in his root, and what all his growth here will come to.

This being done with much seriousness and industry, there must needs follow a great change in man; his understanding will be more and more enlightened, his will more and more conformed to that to which he thus gives himself up. . . . He will find a kind of life and growth in this according to its kind. . . .

Now how easy is it for a man to mistake here, and call this the truth. . . . He sees a change made by this in him, and this he accounts the true conversion and regeneration. . . . Though it may seem to have unity with all the Scriptures in the letter, yet it cannot have unity with one Scripture in the life. . . . So it may have a literal knowledge of the blood of Christ, and of justification; but the life of the blood which livingly justifieth, that birth cannot feel, but can only talk of it, according to the relation it reads in the Scriptures. . . . And here is the great contention in the world between these two births: the one contending for their knowledge in the letter, and the other contending for their knowledge

[8]

in the life; the one setting up their faith from the natural part, calling it spiritual; and the other, who have felt the stroke of God upon this (and thereby come to know the difference), setting up the faith of the true heir.

In plain terms, you must part with all your religion which you have gathered in your own wisdom . . . and which only can make a fair show in the dark but cannot endure the searching light of the day of the Lord, and ye must purchase the true religion, the true righteousness, the true innocency and purity of Christ. The old must be done away, truly done away, and the new come in the place, so that flesh and self may be quite destroyed, and nothing but Christ found in you, and you found nowhere but in Christ, if you enter his kingdom; for no unclean thing can enter. Therefore, put away pride and passion and enmity and fleshly reasonings, and seek out that which is pure, and enter into it, and take up the cross against all that is contrary, that so you may be wrought into it, and found in it . . . and come to that which is infallible. And know the silencing of the fleshly part, that the spiritual part may grow in the wisdom, that so ye may learn in the spirit, and know the word of God, and be able to speak it.

Truth is of God, and was with God, and in God, before anything else had a being. Truth was before error or deceit; for it was from the truth that the error was, and it was about truth that the deceit was. There was somewhat which erred from truth, and brought deceit into the world, and hath propagated deceit in the world; but truth remains the same that it was, keeping its pure, eternal, unchangeable nature, and is not, nor ever was, nor ever can be defiled or tainted with any error or deceit, but testifieth against it, reproveth it;

and condemneth for it, draweth out of it, and delivereth from its bonds and captivity all those that hearken and cleave to it, in the faith which is of its nature and begetting.

Now, is not this a pearl? Nay, is not this the pearl indeed, the precious pearl of price? Who would not buy it? Who would not sell all for it? Who would not dig in the field where this treasure is hid, until he find it? The field is near thee, O man, which thou art to purchase and dig in, and must feel torn up by the plough of God in some measure before this pearl or treasure appear to thee; and thou must take up and bear the yoke and cross of Christ, until all be bowed down and crucified in thee which is contrary to its nature, before it be polished in thee, and thou come to behold and enjoy its riches and everlasting fulness. Oh, happy are they that are begotten and born of it! happy are they that know its voice, and give up to it, to be gathered and redeemed by it, out of all deceits, out of all errors, out of all that entangles and ensnares the soul in sin, misery, and utter perdition; for destruction and misery everlasting is out of it, and life and salvation is alone to be found in it.

Now to the soul that hath felt breathings towards the Lord formerly, and in whom there are yet any true breathings left after his living presence, and after the feeling of his eternal virtue in the heart, I have this to say: "Where art thou? Art thou in thy soul's rest? Dost thou feel the virtue and power of the gospel? Dost thou feel the ease which comes from the living arm, to the heart which is joined to it in the light of the gospel? Is thy laboring for life in a good degree at an end? And dost thou feel the life and power flowing in upon thee

from the free fountain? Is the load really taken off from thy back? Dost thou find the captive redeemed and set free from the power of sin, and the captivity broken, and he which led thee captive from the life and from the eternal power now led captive by the life and by the redeeming power, which is eternal? Hast thou found this, or hast thou missed of it? Let thine heart answer."
Ah! do not imagine and talk away the rest and salvation of thy soul. The gospel state is a state of substance, a state of enjoying the life, a state of feeling the presence and power of the Lord in his pure holy spirit, a state of binding up, a state of healing, a state of knowing the Lord and walking with him in the light of his own spirit. It begins in a sweet, powerful touch of life, and there is a growth in the life (in the power, in the divine virtue, in the rest, peace, and satisfaction of the soul in God) to be administered and waited for daily. Now art thou here, in the living power, in the divine life. joined to the spring of life, drawing water of life out of the well of life with joy? Or art thou dry, dead, barren, sapless, or at best but unsatisfiedly mourning after what thou wantest?

3

THE SEED

THE seed of God is the word of God; the seed of the kingdom is the word of the kingdom. It is a measure of the light and life, of the grace and truth, which is by Jesus Christ, whereof in him is the fulness. It is a heavenly talent, or manifestation of his spirit in the heart, which is given to man for him, in the virtue and strength of Christ, to improve for God. This which God hath placed in man, to witness for himself, and to guide man from evil unto good (in the pure breathings, quickenings, and shinings of it), this is the seed, which is freely bestowed on man, to spring up and remain in him, and to gather him out of himself, into itself.

The pure, living, heavenly knowledge of the Father, and of his Son Christ Jesus, is wrapped up in this seed. God is light; and this seed, which comes from him, is not darkness, but light; and in the springing light of this seed, God and Christ are revealed. The divine nature of them springs up in the seed; . . . yea, here we . . . know the righteous spirit of Christ, the righteous nature of Christ, the righteous life of Christ, and feel him to be one with the Father, who begets of the same spirit, nature, and life in us. And he that is born of the spirit is spirit, and he that is united to the Lord is one spirit; and he that is united to the seed, to the measure of grace and truth from Christ (wherein and whereby the soul is united), is united to God, and ingrafted into Christ; and as the seed is formed in him, Christ is formed in him; and as he is formed and new-created in the seed, he is the workmanship of God, formed and new-created in Christ.

What is the nature of the seed of God, or the seed of the kingdom?

Though the nature of it hath been largely signified already, under the foregoing head, . . . yet I shall speak a little more punctually and expressly of it in several particulars, according to the Scriptures, that the reader may have the more distinct sense and inward apprehension of it, the Lord opening his heart in reading these things.

1. It is of an immortal, incorruptible nature (I Peter i. 23). It is a seed that can never die in itself, though it may be as it were dead in man, or unto man, not putting forth any of its hidden life or virtue in the man that hath slain it as to himself; who, having slain that whereby God gives life, is dead in trespasses and in sins, and cannot live any more, till God breathe upon and quicken this seed in him, and him by this seed. This is a great mystery. Doubtless the seed of life and godliness, wherein the life and godliness of the soul lies hid, must needs be a great mystery, and cannot be known but as God reveals it.

2. It's of a gathering nature. It is of the nature of a net (Matt. xiii. 47). It gathers out of that which is contrary to God, unto God. It gathers out of the world, out of the sea of wickedness, out of the kingdom of darkness, out of a man's own nature and spirit, into God's nature and spirit, and his light and kingdom, wherein the soul should dwell, and walk, and be subject, with God.

3. It is of a purging, cleansing nature. It is of the nature of fire, of the nature of water, inwardly and spiritually. This seed is spirit and life in a measure; and by it, or by God's spirit which dwells and is revealed in it, he washeth and purgeth away the filth of the daughter of Sion, and the blood of Jerusalem from the midst thereof. There is strength in this seed, and virtue in this seed, against all the strength of deceit and wickedness in the other seed; and as it springs up, and is received and joined to in the holy fear of the Lord, it prevails over it, and casteth away its darkness, and purgeth away and burneth up its filth, chaff, and corruption.

4. It is of a seasoning, leavening, sanctifying nature. It is like salt, it is like leaven. It seasons and leavens with life. It seasons and leavens with righteousness. It seasons and leavens with the image of God. So soon as ever it springs in the heart, it begins to leaven it; and if it be not snibbed, or grieved, or hurt, or quenched (for it is of a most sensible, tender nature), it will go on leavening more and more with the nature of truth, into the likeness of the God of truth (Mark ix. 50; Luke xiii. 21; Col. iv. 6).

5. It is of an enriching nature. It is a hidden treasure or pearl of great price. It makes the wise merchant very rich, who sells all for it, and buys the field and it. He that buys the truth, and will by no means sell or part with it, but gives up to it, and makes it his treasure, oh, how doth it enrich his heart with that which is holy and heavenly! How rich doth it make him towards God (Matt. xiii. 44-46)!

6. It is of an improving, growing nature, of a nature that will grow and may be improved. The one talent may be increased into more. The little seed, like a grain of mustard seed, will grow in the good ground beyond

all herbs and become a tree, a tree of righteousness of the Lord's planting, that he may be glorified (Matt. xiii. 31, 32; xxv. 16; viii. 23).

But what need I mention any more? Here is light, here is life, here is righteousness, here is peace, here is heavenly joy, here is the holy power, springing and bringing forth their fruits and precious operations and effects in the heart; and here is assurance of the love of God in Christ forever, and that God will never leave nor forsake that soul which is joined to him, and abides with him in this seed; but it shall be kept by the power of God, through the faith that springs from this seed, unto perfect redemption and salvation. *Amen.*

4

DOCTRINES

NOW, friends, this is an excellent thing indeed to come to and be acquainted with, and receive, that which the Scriptures testify of, to wit, to receive Christ, to feel union with him in his spirit, to enter into the new and holy agreement with God, into the everlasting covenant of life and peace, to feel the partition wall broken down, and the wall of salvation reared up, and the defense which is thereby; to find the law of God, the law of life, the law of the new creation, written in the heart; the pure fear planted there by God, which keepeth the mind and spirit from departing from him; to have his spirit put within, causing to walk in his ways, and to keep his statutes and judgments, and do them; and so to have union and fellowship with the Lord.

For mark the difference between the state of the law and gospel. The law was a shadow of good things to come. The gospel is a state of enjoyment of the good things shadowed out under the law. The law was a type of the kingdom, of the spiritual kingdom of Christ, which is set up under the gospel. In John's day the kingdom was at hand; but in the day of Christ's power the kingdom is come. Under the law there was a tabernacle pitched by man; but under the gospel the true tabernacle and temple is witnessed, which God pitcheth and not man; and the holy, spiritual, heavenly sacrifices, and the living covenant, whereof Christ is the mediator, and the law written in the heart, and the spirit of the Lord put within, so that his presence is as really witnessed inwardly, in that which is truly his tabernacle and temple now, as ever it was witnessed outwardly, in his outward tabernacle and temple under the law.

Thus God did advance the state of a believer above the state of the Jews under the law; for they had the law, though written with the finger of God, yet but in tables of stone; but these have the law, written by the finger of God, in the tables of their hearts. Theirs was a law without, at a distance from them, and the priests' lips were to preserve the knowledge of it and to instruct them in it; but here is a law within, nigh at hand, the immediate light of the spirit of life shining so immediately in the heart that they need no man to teach them, but have the spirit of prophecy in themselves and quick living teachings from him continually, and are made such kings and priests to God as the state of the law did but represent. A Christian is he that comes into this substance of all the shadows contained in the law. A Christian is he that comes into this substance and lives in this substance, and in whom this substance lives. Christ is the substance who lives in the Christian, and he in Christ.

The substance, when it is shadowed out, or when it is nakedly dispensed, is one and the same thing; so that whenever it comes, it cannot be another thing than what the shadow represented it to be. Moses's dispensations and Christ's are one in spirit; and when he cometh in spirit, he doth not destroy either Moses or the prophets, but comprehends them; so that the law is but one, although the dispensations of it have been various.

[17]

What was it that was the thing of great value with the Father, in Christ giving up himself to death? It was his obedience. He did obey his Father in all things, not doing his own will, but the will of him that sent him. He was obedient to death, even the death of the cross. And so, as by one man's disobedience, death came upon all; so by the obedience of one, the free gift came upon all, which free gift is unto life; for life comes upon all that come to him, and believe in him, through the free gift, which is freely tendered to, and come upon all (Rom. v. 18, 19).

Now the Scriptures do expressly distinguish between Christ and the garment which he wore; between him that came, and the body in which he came; between the substance which was veiled, and the veil which veiled it. Lo, I come! A body hast thou prepared me. There is plainly he, and the body in which he came. There was the outward vessel, and the inward life. This we certainly know, and can never call the bodily garment Christ, but that which appeared and dwelt in the body. Now if ye indeed know the Christ of God, tell us plainly what that is which appeared in the body? Whether that was not the Christ before it took up the body, after it took up the body, and forever?

As touching free will, we know, from God, that man in his fallen estate is spiritually dead, and hath no free will to good; but his understanding and will are both darkened and captivated by the enemy. But in Christ there is freedom, and in his word there is power and life, and that reaching to the heart, looseneth the bands of the enemy, and begetteth not only a freedom of mind towards good, but an inclination, desires, and breathings

[18]

after it. Thus the Father draws; and thus the soul (feeling the drawing) answers in some measure; and the soul, thus coming, is welcomed by Christ, and accepted of the Father.

There is predestination, election, calling, justifying, glorifying: predestination unto holiness, election in that which is holy, calling out of darkness into light, justifying and glorifying in the light, through the renewing and sanctification of the Spirit. All these God ordereth and manageth according to his good will, and according as he hath purposed in himself; although he be not the decreer, nor author of sin or rebellion against himself, which is the cause of the creature's condemnation.

Christ is a perfect physician, and is able to work a perfect cure on the heart that believeth in him, and waiteth upon him. Yea, he came to destroy the works of the devil, to cleanse man's mind of the darkness and power of Satan, and to fill it with the life and power of truth; and he sent forth a ministry not only for the beginning, but for the perfecting of the work: yea, his word in the mouth and heart is powerful, sharper than a two-edged sword, and he can cast out the strong man, and cut down all that is corrupt and contrary to himself, and break down every stronghold in the mind, and spoil all the goods of the enemy. Christ likewise bids his disciples be perfect, as their heavenly Father is perfect; and the apostle bids men perfect holiness in the fear of God, that they might be fully separated from, and not so much as touch, the unclean thing; but enjoy the promises of God's dwelling in them, and walking in them, whose temple under the gospel is to be pure.

In the state of perfection, the blood is not laid aside

as useless, but remains to keep pure for ever. It is the blood of the everlasting covenant. . . . Both the covenant and the blood last for ever, and are useful even to them that are perfect. And there is need and use of the faith in the blood, to believe the preservation. As the covenant itself lasts, so that which lets into and keeps in the covenant lasts also. That which unites and ties the soul to Christ the life, abides in the soul for ever, even as the union itself abides. And there is a growing in the life, even where the heart is purified from sin, even as Christ did grow and wax strong in spirit; for a state of perfection doth not exclude degrees. And so there is also a need of watching against temptations in a perfect state; for Adam was perfect, and yet he needed a watch: and Christ was perfectly pure and without sin and yet He did both watch and pray.

5

THE YOKE

THAT Christ's immediate revelation of the nature of his Father is to his babes, not to the wise, not to the zealous, not to the studious, not to the devout, not to the rich in the knowledge of the Scriptures without, but to the weak, the foolish, the poor, the lowly in heart. And man receives not these revelations by study, by reading, by willing, by running, but by being formed in the will of life, by being begotten of the will of the Father, and by coming forth in the will, and lying still in the will, and growing up in the will. Here the child receives the wisdom which is from above, and daily learns that cross which crucifies the other wisdom, which joins with and pleases the other will, which loves to be feeding on the shadowy and husky part of knowledge, without life.

Strait is the gate, narrow is the way, that leadeth unto life, and few there be that find it. The way of unbelief is broad, yea, the way of belief is broad also. It is easy for a man so to believe concerning Christ, or in Christ (as his heart may call it), as to miss of the nature of the true faith, and of the sweet and blessed effects which accompany it. It is easy likewise to miss the yoke (to take up a wrong yoke, in the self-will, self-wisdom, self-interpretation of Scriptures), or easy starting aside from the true yoke; but it is hard coming under the yoke of the life, and hard abiding under it. Again, it is easy mis-learning: a man may so read, and so hear, as that he may be always learning, and never come to the knowledge of the truth; never come to the truth as it is received and held in Jesus, but may so get and hold the knowledge of the truth, as man in his wisdom may get and hold it from the letter. And if a man thus miss the way, how can he attain the end? If a man begin not in the true faith, in the living faith, how can he attain the rest which the true faith alone leads to? If a man miss of the yoke, or abide not constantly under the yoke, how can he meet with the true ease and rest which is in it, and which it alone can administer? If a man learn not the truth aright of the true teacher, how can he ever reap the effects of the true knowledge?

Christ hath plainly chalked out the path of his rest to every weary, panting soul, which he that walketh in cannot miss of. He hath cast up, cast up; he hath made the way plain in the gospel, so plain that the wayfaring man, though a fool, yet keeping to the light of the gospel, cannot err therein, or miss of the blessed rest thereof. How is it? Why, come unto me; take my yoke upon you, and learn of me. He that walketh in this path cannot miss of it: the rest is at the end of it, nay, the rest is in it: he that believeth entereth into the rest. The true faith, the faith which stands in the power, and which is given to the birth which is born from above, is the substance of the rest hoped for, and there is a true taste and some enjoyment of it given to him that truly believeth.

What is love? What shall I say of it, or how shall I in words express its nature? It is the sweetness of life;

it is the sweet, tender, melting nature of God, flowing up through his seed of life into the creature, and of all things making the creature most like unto himself, both in nature and operation. It fulfills the law, it fulfills the gospel; it wraps up all in one, and brings forth all in the oneness. It excludes all evil out of the heart, it perfects all good in the heart. A touch of love doth this in measure; perfect love doth this in fulness. But how can I proceed to speak of it? Oh, that the souls of all that fear and wait on the Lord might feel its nature fully, and then would they not fail of its sweet, over-coming operations, both towards one another, and towards enemies. The great healing, the great conquest, the great salvation is reserved for the full manifestation of the love of God. His judgments, his cuttings, his hewings by the word of his mouth are but to prepare for, but not to do, the great work of raising up the sweet building of his life, which is to be done in love, and in peace, and by the power thereof. And this my soul waits and cries after, even the full springing up of eternal love in my heart, and in the swallowing of me wholly into it, and the bringing of my soul wholly forth in it, that the life of God in its own perfect sweetness may freely run forth through this vessel, and not be at all tinctured by the vessel, but perfectly tincture and change the vessel into its own nature; and then shall no fault be found in my soul before the Lord, but the spotless life be fully enjoyed by me, and become a perfectly pleasant sacrifice to my God.

Oh, how sweet is love! How pleasant is its nature! How takingly doth it behave itself in every condition, upon every occasion, to every person, and about every-thing! How tenderly, how readily, doth it help and serve the meanest! How patiently, how meekly, doth it bear all things, either from God or man, how unexpectedly soever they come, or how hard soever they seem! How doth it believe, how doth it hope, how doth it excuse, how doth it cover even that which seemeth not to be excusable, and not fit to be covered! How kind is it even in its interpretations and charges concerning miscarriages! It never over-chargeth, it never grates upon the spirit of him whom it reprehends; it never hardens, it never provokes; but carrieth a meltingness and power of conviction with it. This is the nature of God; this, in the vessels capacitated to receive and bring it forth in its glory, the power of enmity is not able to stand against, but falls before, and is overcome by.

That poverty and humility of spirit, which springeth from the same root from which the faith, the love, the peace, the joy, and the other heavenly things arise, and is of the same nature. There is a voluntary humility, and a voluntary poverty, even of spirit, which man casts himself into, and forms in himself, by his own workings and reasonings. This is not the true, but the false image, or counterfeit of the true; but then there is a poverty which ariseth from God's emptying the creature, from God's stripping the creature; and a humility which ariseth from a new heart and nature. This is of the right kind, and is lasting, and abides in the midst of the riches and glory of the kingdom. For as Christ was poor in spirit before his Father, and lowly in heart in the midst of all the fulness which he received from him; so it is with those who are of the same birth and nature with Christ. They are filled with humility and clothed with humility, in the midst of all the graces and heavenly riches which God fills them and adorns them with. Keep in the faith, keep in the truth, keep in the light, keep in the power. It excludes boasting in or after the flesh, and keeps the mind in that humility and poverty of spirit which God hath brought, and daily further and further brings, it into. And so the humility and poverty remains (poor in spirit for ever, humble in spirit for ever, nothing before the Lord for ever), even as that remains which brought into that frame, and keeps in that frame forever. And so the Lord of Life is only exalted, and the creature kept abased before him, and low forever; and is nothing but as the Lord pleaseth to fill, and make it to be what it is.

6

WORSHIP

AND this is the manner of their worship. They are to wait upon the Lord, to meet in the silence of flesh, and to watch for the stirrings of his life, and the breakings forth of his power amongst them. And in the breakings forth of that power they may pray, speak, exhort, rebuke, sing, or mourn, and so on, according as the spirit teaches, requires, and gives utterance. But if the spirit do not require to speak, and give to utter, then everyone is to sit still in his place (in his heavenly place I mean) feeling his own measure, feeding thereupon, receiving therefrom (into his spirit) what the Lord giveth. Now in this is edifying, pure edifying, precious edifying; his soul who thus waits is hereby particularly edified by the spirit of the Lord at every meeting. And then also there is the life of the whole felt in every vessel that is turned to its measure; insomuch as the warmth of life in each vessel doth not only warm the particular, but they are like an heap of fresh and living coals, warming one another, insomuch as a great strength, freshness, and vigor of life flows into all. And if any be burthened, tempted, buffeted by Satan, bowed down, overborne, languishing, afflicted, distressed, and so on, the estate of such is felt in spirit, and secret cries or open (as the Lord pleaseth), ascend up to the Lord for them, and they many times find ease and relief, in a few words spoken, or without words, if it be the season of their help and relief with the Lord.

For absolutely silent meetings (wherein there is a resolution not to speak) we know not; but we wait on the Lord, either to feel him in words, or in silence of spirit without words, as he pleaseth. And that which we aim at, and are instructed to by the spirit of the Lord as to silent meetings, is that the flesh in everyone be kept silent, and that there be no building up, but in the spirit and power of the Lord.

Our worship is a deep exercise of our spirits before the Lord, which doth not consist in an exercising the natural part or natural mind, either to hear or speak words, or in praying according to what we, of ourselves, can apprehend or comprehend concerning our needs; but we wait, in silence of the fleshly part, to hear with the new ear what God shall please to speak inwardly in our own hearts, or outwardly through others, who speak with the new tongue which he unlooseth and teacheth to speak; and we pray in the spirit, and with the new understanding, as God pleaseth to quicken, draw forth, and open our hearts towards himself.

Thus our minds being gathered into the measure, or gift of grace, which is by Jesus Christ; here we appear before our God, and here our God, and his Christ, is witnessed in the midst of us.

This is that gathering in the name, which the promise is to, where we meet together, waiting with one consent on the Father of Life, bowing and confessing to him in the name of his Son; and that fleshly part, that fleshly understanding, that fleshly wisdom, that fleshly will, which will not bow, is chained down, and kept under by the power of life which God stretcheth forth over it, and subdueth it by. So then, there is the sweet communion enjoyed, the sweet love flowing, the sweet peace of spirit reaped, which the Father breathes upon, and gives to his children; the sweet joy and refreshment in the Lord our righteousness, who causeth righteousness to drop down from heaven, and truth to spring up out of the earth. And so our Father is felt blessing us, blessing our land, blessing our habitations, delighting in us and over us to do us good; and our land yields its increase to the Lord of Life, who hath redeemed it and planted the precious plants and seeds of life in it.

Give over thine own willing, give over thine own running, give over thine own desiring to know or be anything, and sink down to the seed which God sows in thy heart and let that be in thee, and grow in thee, and breathe in thee, and act in thee, and thou shalt find by sweet experience that the Lord knows that and loves and owns that, and will lead it to the inheritance of life, which is his portion.

Lord, take care of all thy children. Oh, thou tender Father, consider what they suffer for the testimony of thy truth, and for thy name's sake, and uphold them, and give them victory, and a holy dominion over all, because it belongs to thy seed into which thou hast gathered them, and in which thou hast united them to thyself. Oh, carry on thy glorious work, which thy own mighty arm hath begun, and cut it short in righteousness for thine Elect's sake, that it may be finished by thee, to thine own everlasting praise. Thy children wait on thee, they cry to thee day and night, that they may be preserved by thee in the well-doing, and in the pure, holy, innocent sufferings for thy truth's sake; until thou say, "It is enough," until thy Holy Spirit say, "It is finished, my lambs, ye shall suffer no more, but now ye shall reign with me and my Son for ever."

Christ is the minister of the true sanctuary, which God hath pitched, and not man. There is a city whose builder and maker is God. The foundation stone, the cornerstone, the top stone of this city or building is Christ. He, therefore, that would know Christ, and be built upon Christ, must find a holy thing revealed in his heart, and his soul built thereon by him who alone can raise this building, who can rear up the tabernacle that hath long been fallen down, who can build up the old waste places, and restore the paths for the ransomed and redeemed of the Lord to walk and travel on in.

Therefore the great work of the minister of Christ is to keep the conscience open to Christ, and to preserve men from receiving any truths of Christ as from them further than the spirit opens, or to imitate any of their practices further than the spirit leads, guides, and persuades them. For persons are exceeding prone to receive things as truths from those whom they have a high opinion of, and to imitate their practices, and so hurt their own growth and endanger their souls. For if I receive a truth before the Lord, by his spirit, make it manifest to me, I lose my guide and follow but the counsel of the flesh, which is exceeding greedy of receiving truths and running into religious practices without the spirit. Therefore the main thing in religion is to keep the conscience pure to the Lord, to know the guide, to follow the guide, to receive from him the light whereby I am to walk; and not to take things for truths because others see them to be truths, but to wait till the spirit make them manifest to me; nor to run into worships, duties, performances, or practices, because others are led thither, but to wait till the spirit lead me thither. He that makes haste to be rich (even in religion, running into knowledge, and into worships and performances, before he feel a true and clear guidance) shall not be innocent; nor the Lord will not hold him guiltless, when he comes to visit, for spiritual adultery and idolatry.

He that keeps not a day, may unite in the same spirit, in the same life, in the same love with him that keeps a day; and he who keeps a day, may unite in heart and soul with the same spirit and life in him who keeps not a day; but he that judgeth the other because of either of these, errs from the spirit, from the love, from the life, and so breaks the bond of unity. And he that draws another to any practice before the life in his own particular lead him doth, as much as in him lies, destroy the soul of that person.

Let nothing judge in thee (concerning thine own heart, or concerning others, or concerning any way or truth of God) but only the begotten of God in the heart. Let the light in which thou art begotten to God, and which shines upon his begotten, be the only judge in thee, and then thou canst not err in judgment. Be not hasty, be not forward in judgment, keep back to the life, still waiting for the appearance and openings of the life. A few steps fetched in the life and power of God are much safer and sweeter than a hasty progress in the hasty forward spirit.

True obedience, gospel obedience, flows from life, flows from the living faith. If I could obey in all things that God requires of me, yet that would not satisfy me, unless I felt my obedience flow from the birth of His life in me. "My Father doth all in me," saith Christ.

This was Christ's comfort. And to feel Christ do all in the soul is the comfort of everyone that truly believes in him.

Canst thou pray? How camest thou to learn to pray? Wast thou taught from above? Or didst thou gain the skill and ability by the exercise and improvement of thine own natural part? Didst thou begin with sighs and groans, staying there till the same spirit that taught thee to groan, taught thee also to speak? Wast thou ever able to distinguish the sighs and groans of the spirit's begetting from the sighs and groans of thy own natural and affectionate part?

Prayer is the breath of the living child to the Father of Life, in that spirit which quickened it, which giveth it the right sense of its wants, and suitable cries proportionable to its state, in the proper season thereof. So that mark: Prayer is wholly out of the will of the creature; wholly out of the time of the creature; wholly out of the power of the creature; in the spirit of the Father, who is the fountain of life, and giveth forth breathings of life to his child at his pleasure.

7

TESTIMONIES

THE works that flow from God's good spirit, the works that are wrought in God, they are good works; the works of the new birth, of the new creature, are good works; whereas all the works of the flesh are bad, though never so finely painted. All its thoughts, imaginations, reasonings, willings, runnings, hunting to find out God and heavenly things, with all its sacrifices, are corrupt and evil, having of the bad leaven, of the bad nature in them. Make the tree good, or its fruit can never be good; so that they are only the good works that flow from the good tree, from the good root.

There is a continual praying unto God. There is a continual blessing and praising of his name, in eating, or drinking, or whatever else is done. There is a continual bowing to the majesty of the Lord in every thought, in every word, in every action, though it be in worldly things and occasions; yet the spirit of the Lord is seen there, and the tongue confesseth him there, and the knee boweth to him there. This is the true worship, and this is the rest or Sabbath wherein the true worshippers worship.

The church is called into the liberty of the gospel, and her children are born of the word immortal, and of the truth which makes free; and it is not the church's nature either to receive or impose yokes of bondage, but to stand fast, and to exhort all her members to stand fast, in the liberty wherewith Christ hath made them free. But where there is any thing unruly, or contrary to the power, that is to be yoked down by the power.

And the particular waiting upon God in his Holy Spirit, light, and power, the spirit, light, and power, will discover what is disorderly, and unruly, and not of God in the particular, and lay a yoke upon it. The church also waiting upon God, in their meetings together in his name, the Lord will discover what is hurtful to the body, and contrary to the life of the body, and lay yokes upon it; and he that refuseth this yoke, keeps alive that which is impure and fleshly, and keeps down the just in himself.

There are some considerations springing up in my heart concerning unity . . . which are as follows:

Unity in the spiritual body, which is gathered into and knit together in the pure life, is a most natural and comely thing. Yea, it is exceeding lovely to find all that are of the Lord of one heart, of one mind, of one judgment, in one way of practice and order in all things.

The Lord is to be waited upon for the bringing forth of this in the body; that as there is a foundation of it laid in all (the life and spring being over all), so all may be brought by him into the true and full oneness.

The Lord is to be acknowledged and praised in the bringing of it forth (so far as it is brought forth), and to be waited upon for the further perfecting of it.

A watch is to be kept (throughout the whole body, and in every heart) for the preserving of it, so far as it is brought forth, that the enemy, by no device or subtility, cause disunion or difference in any respect, wherein there was once a true unity and oneness. For the enemy will watch to divide; and if he be not watched against, in that which is able to discover and keep him out, by some device or other he will take his advantage to make a rent (in those that are not watchful) from the pure truth and unity of life in the body. For he that in the least thing rents from the body (in any respect or particular which was brought forth by the life), he in that respect hearkens to another spirit (even the dividing spirit) and by its instigation rents from the life itself, and so doth not keep his habitation, nor his unity, with that which abides in its habitation.

He which is born of God, he who is of the love, and in the love, cannot but be tender. He who is born of the earthly wisdom, who taketh up and holdeth forth a religion there, cannot but persecute. Why so? Because he cannot but judge that any man may take up religion as he hath done, and so, by reasonings, may come to acknowledge and take up what he hath taken up, and holdeth forth, or else he is wilful and stubborn, as he judgeth. But now he that is born of God, and hath received his light, knowledge, religion, and way of worship from him, he knoweth that no man can rightly receive them but the same way, to wit, from God, by the light which he causeth to shine into the heart at his pleasure, and in the faith which he gives. So that God's free and powerful spirit is to be waited upon, for the working of all in his people, and not any forced to act beyond, or contrary to, the principle of his life and light in them.

Yet the government of Christ and his kingdom is not

opposite to any just government of a nation or people. Christ's government is a righteous government of the heart, or inner man, chiefly; which doth not oppose a righteous government of the outward man. Nay, those who are Christ's subjects, and singly obedient to his law of righteousness in their spirits, are more faithful to men, and more subject to any just law of government, than others can be; for their fidelity and subjection is out of love, and for conscience sake. But this is which offends the world; men many times make laws in their own will, and according to their own wisdom (now the wisdom of the world is corrupt, and hath erred from the guidance of God), and are not free from self-ends and interests, not being gathered into that which cleanseth and keepeth pure the naturals. Now that which is of God cannot bow to any thing which is corrupt in man. It can lie down and suffer, and bear the plowing of long and deep furrows upon its back; but it cannot act that which is against its life. It cannot be disloyal to its king, to gratify the spirit of this world; but what practice or testimony its king calls for against the evil and corruption of this world, it must obey singly and faithfully.

As government came from God, so the righteous execution of it depends upon God. Every man needs God's help daily, else he may easily err in his course; and governments and governors need God's help much more, in the many intricacies and perplexities which they often meet with. And God is nigh to them in their difficult cases, who wait upon him for counsel and direction. If the case be knotty, yet if God give wisdom, hath the magistrate cause to complain? And will not the Lord assist that magistrate, who in his fear waits on him, and is not willing to spare the evil, and afraid to hurt the good? If there were not so much consulting with man's wisdom and policy (nor such laying of designs and intents at first as spring from man and not from God), but a naked, upright waiting on him for instruction, who can only guide the spirit of man aright, governments would not prove so difficult, nor the success therein so dangerous.

Their way of determining things at last (which is by a vote of the major part) is an uncertain way of determination; for it is not impossible that the major part may be over-swayed by by-ends, and in relation to their own advantage and interest, against the righteousness and equity of the reason of the lesser part; so that the way of determining things by a council is not a certain way in itself: but because men know not well how to find out a better and more probable way of deciding controversies, they judge it necessary to acquiesce therein. But the votes and determinations of men concerning a thing do not conclude a thing to be true or false in itself; they only signify their opinion, judgment, and testimony concerning the thing. . . .

The dictate of conscience is not made a plea by us, but the answering and obeying the light of Christ in our consciences is that which keepeth them void of offence, both towards God and towards men. Now it is one thing for a man to act evil, and plead it is his conscience; and it is another thing for a man to be guided by the infallible light of the spirit; or, if he be not come so far, yet to be made tender in his heart towards Christ concerning his practices in religion. In this last case we say that in things whose good or evil chiefly depends upon the knowledge and persuasion of the mind, which Christ alone can do, here Christ is the sole lord and judge of the conscience (Rom. xiv, 4), and not either minister, church, or magistrate. Christ giveth knowledge, Christ increaseth knowledge, and Christ requireth obedience according to the knowledge given or increased.

Fighting is not suitable to a gospel spirit; but to the spirit of the world, and the children thereof. The fighting in the gospel is turned inward against the lusts, and not outward against the creatures. There is to be a time when nation shall not lift up sword against nation, neither shall they learn war any more. When the power of the gospel spreads over the whole earth, thus shall it be throughout the earth; and where the power of the spirit takes hold of and overcomes any heart at present, thus will it be at present with that heart. This blessed state, which shall be brought forth in the general in God's season, must begin in particulars; and they therein are not prejudicial to the world (nor would be so looked upon, if the right eye in man were but open to see with), but emblems of that blessed state which the God of glory hath promised to set up in the world in the days of the gospel.

Israel of old stood not by their strength and wisdom and preparations against their enemies, but in quietness and confidence and waiting on the Lord for direction, and shall not such now, who are true Israelites, and have indeed attained to the true gospel state, follow the Lord in the peaceable life and spirit of the gospel unless they see by rational demonstration beforehand how they shall be preserved therein? I speak not this against any magistrate's or people's defending themselves against foreign invasions, or making use of the sword to suppress the violent and evildoers within their borders (for this the present estate of things may and doth require, and a great blessing will attend the sword where it is borne uprightly to that end, and its use will be honorable; and while there is need of a sword, the Lord will not suffer that government, or those governors, to want fitting instruments under them for the managing thereof, to wait on him in his fear to have the edge of it rightly directed). But yet there is a better state, which the Lord hath already brought some into, and which nations are to expect and travel towards. Yea, it is far better to know the Lord to be the defender, and to wait on him daily, and see the need of his strength, wisdom, and preservation, than to be ever so strong and skilful in weapons of war.

This, then, is the sum of our answer in this respect: we are not against the true life and power of godliness, wherever it hath appeared, or yet appears, under the veil of any form whatsoever. Nay, all persons who singly wait upon the Lord in the simplicity and sincerity of their hearts, whether under any form, or out of forms (that matters little to us), are very dear unto us in the Lord. But we are against all forms, images, imitations, and appearances which betray the simplicity and sincerity of the heart, keep the life in bondage, and endanger the loss of the soul. And too many such now there are, which hold the immortal seed of life in captivity under death, over which we cannot but mourn, and wait for its breaking off the chains, and its rising out of all its graves into its own pure life, power, and fulness of liberty in the Lord.

8

CONCLUSION

AND so at length we came to witness (abiding the
trial of this dreadful day, wherein our God appeared to us as a consuming fire) a new heaven and a
new earth inwardly; and no more sea of wickedness, no
more sea of inward trouble, but righteousness, peace,
and joy inwardly and our God becoming a rich portion
to us, watching over us in most tender care and love,
and delighting in us to do us good, making known to
us the riches of the gospel, even the feast of fat things;
and giving us to partake of the well or fountain of
living waters in our own hearts, which springs up fresh-
ly in us daily unto life eternal. So that we were not only
invited to the waters, but taught also to come thereto;
and when we came, we were not sent away empty, but
had the water of life given us; which became such a well
as out of it flow streams of living water. Ah, blessed be
the Lord! Did we ever think, in our dry, dead, barren estate, to have seen such a day as this?

All people upon earth who love your souls, and have
any true secret pantings after God, look to the nature
of your spirits, and look to the nature of those things
ye let into your minds; lest ye take death for life, error
for truth, and so sow to yourselves corruption and rear
up a fabric in Mystery Babylon, which will be turned

into desolation and utter ruins by the power of life from Sion.

Propositions concerning the Only Way of Salvation:

That there is no way of being saved from sin, and wrath eternal, but by that Christ alone who died at Jerusalem. . . .

That there is no way of being saved by him, but through receiving him into the heart by a living faith, and having him formed in the heart. . . .

That there is no way of receiving Christ into the heart and of having him formed there, but by receiving the light of his spirit, in which light he is and dwells. . . .

That the way of receiving the light of the spirit into the heart is by hearkening to, and receiving, its convictions of sin there.

How faith, or believing in the light, worketh out the salvation:

It causeth a fear and trembling to seize upon the sinner. The Lord God Almighty, by the rising of his light in the heart, causeth the powers of darkness to shake . . . and then the plant of the Lord springs up out of the dry and barren ground. . . .

In this fear and trembling the work of true repentance and conversion is begun and carried on. There is a turning of the soul from the darkness to the light; from the dark power to the light power; from the spirit of deceit to the spirit of truth; from all false appearances and imaginations about holiness to that which the eternal light manifesteth to be truly so. And now is a time of mourning, of deep mourning, while the separation is working, while the enemy's strength is not broken and subdued, and the heart is now and then feeling itself still hankering after its old lovers.

In the belief of the light . . . there springs up a hope, a living hope. . . . It stays the soul in all the troubles, storms, and tempests it meets afterwards, which are many, yea, very many.

Faith through hope works righteousness, and teaches the true wisdom; and now the benefit of all the former trouble, anguish, and misery begins to be felt and the work goes on sweetly. . . .

In the righteousness, and in the true wisdom which is received in the light, there springs up a love, and a unity, and fellowship with God the Father of Lights, and with all who are children of the light. . . . And here is a willingness and power felt in this love to lay down the life even for the least truth of Christ's, or for the brethren.

Belief in the light works patience, meekness, gentleness, tenderness, and long-suffering. It will bear anything for God, anything for men's souls' sake. It will wait quietly and stilly for the carrying on of the work of God in its own soul, and for the manifestation of God's love and mercy to others. It will bear the contradiction and reproach of sinners, seeking their good, even while they are plotting, contriving, and hatching mischief, laying many subtile snares. . . .

It brings peace, joy, and glory. . . . And this is the true peace, and certain peace. . . . Here is joy, unspeakable joy, joy which the world cannot see or touch, nor the powers of darkness come near to interrupt . . . and this joy is full of glory, which glory increaseth daily more and more, by the daily sight and feeling of the living virtue and power in Christ the light, whereby the soul is continually transformed, and changed more and more out of the corruptible into the incorruptible. . . .

Here, in the light, I meet with certainty, assurance, satisfaction, yea, infallibility. I meet with the evidence and demonstration of God's spirit, which is infallible. I meet with God's witness, which is an infallible witness. I meet with God's spirit, which is an infallible spirit, who infallibly leads into all truth, and infallibly guides in the truth. I meet with an infallible shepherd, who hath an infallible voice, and gives to his sheep an infallible ear, wherewith they infallibly hear. He opens an infallible eye, and gives to it an infallible sight of God, and the heavenly mysteries of his kingdom. The spirit breathes infallibly, begets infallibly, leads infallibly, creates a new heart, a right spirit; which heart, which spirit, is of God's infallible nature, like him; for that which is born of the spirit is spirit.

But some may desire to know what I have at last met with. I answer, I have met with the seed. Understand that word, and thou wilt be satisfied, and enquire no further. I have met with my God; I have met with my Savior; and he hath not been present with me without his salvation; but I have felt the healings drop upon my soul from under his wings. I have met with the true knowledge, the knowledge of life, the living knowledge, the knowledge which is life; and this hath had the true virtue in it, which my soul hath rejoiced in, in the presence of the Lord. I have met with the seed's Father, and in the seed I have felt him my Father. There I have read his nature, his love, his compassions, his tenderness, which have melted, overcome, and changed my heart before him. I have met with the seed's faith, which hath done and doth that which the faith of man can never do. I have met with the true birth, with the birth which is heir of the kingdom, and inherits the kingdom.

I have met with the true spirit of prayer and supplication, wherein the Lord is prevailed with, and which draws from him whatever the condition needs; the soul always looking up to him in the will, and in the time and way, which is acceptable with him. What shall I say? I have met with the true peace, the true righteousness, the true holiness, the true rest of the soul, the everlasting habitation which the redeemed dwell in; and I know all these to be true, in him that is true, and am capable of no doubt, dispute, or reasoning in my mind about them; it abiding there, where it hath received the full assurance and satisfaction. And also I know very well and distinctly in spirit where the doubts and disputes are, and where the certainty and full assurance is, and in the tender mercy of the Lord am preserved out of the one, and in the other.